# SUMMER MATH WORKBOOK

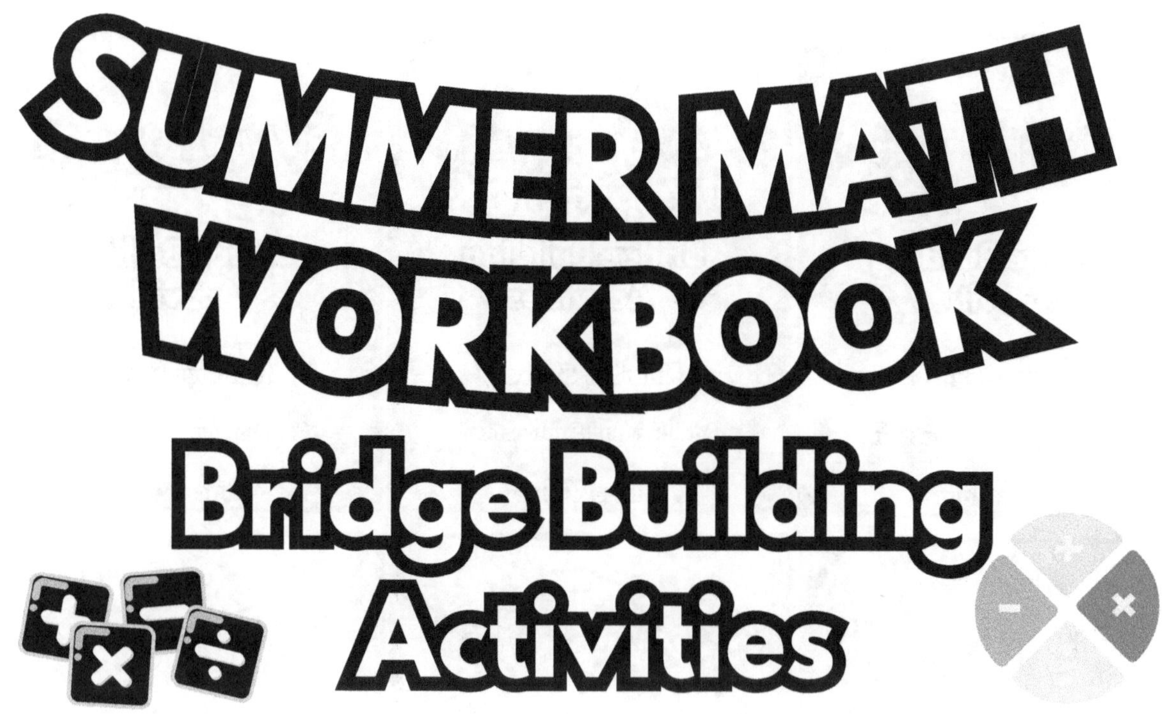


## Bridge Building Activities

| Grade 1 → 2 | Grade 2 → 3 | Grade 3 → 4 |
|---|---|---|
| **SUMMER MATH WORKBOOK** | **SUMMER MATH WORKBOOK** | **SUMMER MATH WORKBOOK** |
| Bridge Building Activities | Bridge Building Activities | Bridge Building Activities |
| Number Sense | Number Sense | Number Sense |
| Addition and Subtraction | Addition and Subtraction | Addition and Subtraction |
| Place Value | Place Value | Place Value |

| Grade 4 → 5 | Grade 5 → 6 | Grade 6 → 7 |
|---|---|---|
| **SUMMER MATH WORKBOOK** | **SUMMER MATH WORKBOOK** | **SUMMER MATH WORKBOOK** |
| Bridge Building Activities | Bridge Building Activities | Bridge Building Activities |
| Multiplication and Division | Multiplication and Division | Arithmetic |
| Place Value and Units | Factors and Multiples | Algebra |
| Fractions and Geometry | Fractions and Geometry | Geometry and Statistics |

| Grade 7 → 8 | Grade 8 → 9 | Grade 9 → 10 |
|---|---|---|
| **SUMMER MATH WORKBOOK** | **SUMMER MATH WORKBOOK** | **SUMMER MATH WORKBOOK** |
| Bridge Building Activities | Bridge Building Activities | Bridge Building Activities |
| Ratio and Percentage | Ratio and Percentage | Factoring and Distributing |
| Algebra and Cartesian Plane | Algebra | Algebra |
| Geometry and Statistics | Geometry and Graphing | Geometry and Graphing |

# Introduction

As parents and educators, we understand the pivotal role that mathematics plays in shaping a child's academic journey and future success. Yet, the path to mathematical proficiency can often seem daunting, filled with challenges and complexities. That's where the transformative power of Summer Bridge Building Activities books comes into play, illuminating the way forward with clarity, precision, and purpose.

Summer vacation is a time for rest and relaxation, but it also presents the risk of the "summer slide," where students lose some of the academic gains they made during the school year. Summer Bridge Building Activities books are specifically designed to tackle this challenge, ensuring that your child stays academically engaged and prepared for the upcoming school year. These books provide a seamless bridge from one grade to the next, reinforcing essential skills and introducing new concepts that will give your child a head start.

Imagine your child eagerly diving into the pages of a Summer Bridge Building Activities book, greeted by clear, engaging content that demystifies complex mathematical concepts. With each turn of the pages, they embark on a journey of discovery, encountering thoughtfully curated practice questions that reinforce learning and sharpen problem-solving skills. As they unveil the answers to those questions, a sense of accomplishment blossoms within them — a tangible reward for their hard work and dedication.

Summer Bridge Building Activities books transcend traditional educational tools; they are meticulously crafted to build a deep and enduring understanding of mathematics. These books follow a sequential and logical progression, starting from fundamental principles and advancing to sophisticated problem-solving strategies. Each chapter is designed to build on the previous one, ensuring a solid and comprehensive foundation for future learning.

Parents, we yearn for nothing more than to see our children thrive academically and personally. We want to witness the spark of inspiration ignited within them as they overcome academic challenges with confidence and poise. Summer Bridge Building Activities books serve as indispensable partners in this noble endeavor, offering not just practice questions but the keys to unlocking a world of academic and personal opportunities.

Visualize the pride on your child's face as they master a challenging math concept, the joy they experience when their efforts yield results, and the confidence they gain with each success. These pages are designed to make learning math a positive, enriching, and deeply rewarding experience that will benefit them throughout their academic journey and beyond.

For educators, Summer Bridge Building Activities books are invaluable allies in the quest to cultivate mathematical proficiency in the classroom. Accompanied by comprehensive guides and readily available answers, instructors can focus on mentoring and nurturing their students, secure in the knowledge that these books provide a robust framework for effective learning.

Within the pages of Summer Bridge Building Activities books lies not just the promise of academic excellence, but the seeds of a brighter future. By integrating these resources into your child's summer routine, you are bestowing upon them the gifts of confidence, curiosity, and a lifelong love of learning.

Invest in your child's future today with Summer Bridge Building Activities books — because every great journey begins with a single step, and this step can change everything. Keep the momentum of learning alive over the summer, and watch your child soar to new academic heights.

#  Contents

Grade 7-9
PRE ALGEBRA WORKBOOK
BRIDGE BUILDING
ACTIVITIES
Equations, Inequalities and Expressions
Linear Equations Graphing and Slope
System of Equations Quadratic Equations

Grade 6-8
PRE ALGEBRA WORKBOOK
BRIDGE BUILDING
ACTIVITIES
Equations One Side and Two Sides
Verbal Algebra Expressions
Linear Equations and Slope Order of Operations

Grade 5-6
PRE ALGEBRA WORKBOOK
BRIDGE BUILDING
ACTIVITIES
Integers, Mixed Numbers Decimals and Fractions
Place Value Exponents and Roots
Percentage and Ratio Word Problems

PRE ALGEBRA WORKBOOK
for Beginners
Integers Fractions, Mixed Numbers
Place Value Exponents and Roots
Percentage Ratio Conversion

PRE ALGEBRA WORKBOOK
for Adults
Integers Percent and Ratio
Equations, Inequalities Expressions
Order of Operations

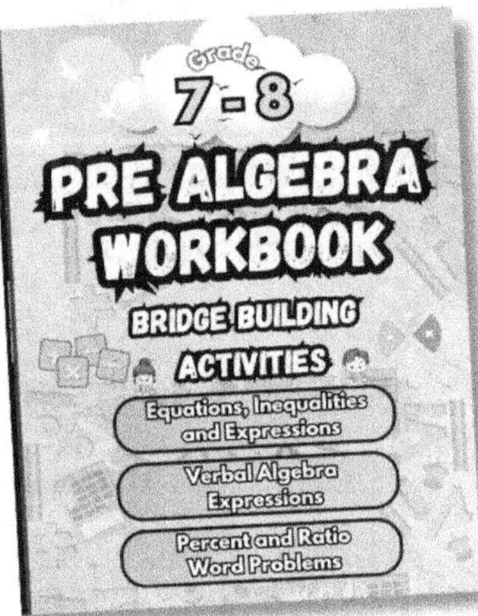

Grade 7-8
PRE ALGEBRA WORKBOOK
BRIDGE BUILDING
ACTIVITIES
Equations, Inequalities and Expressions
Verbal Algebra Expressions
Percent and Ratio Word Problems

Grade 9-10
PRE ALGEBRA WORKBOOK
BRIDGE BUILDING
ACTIVITIES
Equations and Inequalities Verbal Algebra
Linear and Quadratic Equations
System of Equations Polynomials

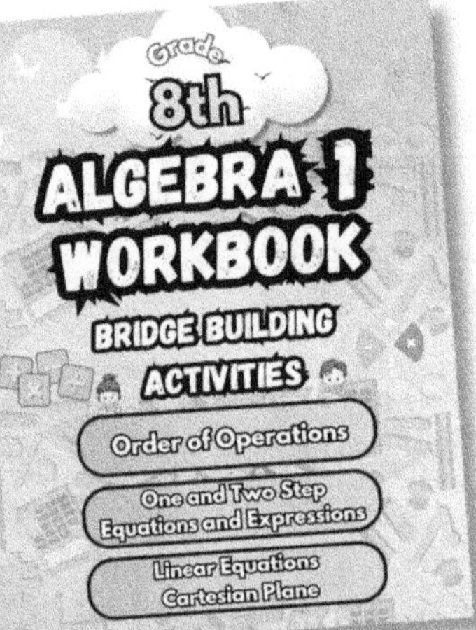

Grade 8th
ALGEBRA 1 WORKBOOK
BRIDGE BUILDING
ACTIVITIES
Order of Operations
One and Two Step Equations and Expressions
Linear Equations Cartesian Plane

Grade 7-9
ALGEBRA 1 WORKBOOK
BRIDGE BUILDING
ACTIVITIES
Integers Order of Operations
One and Multi Step Equations and Expressions
Linear, Quadratic Equations Equations One Side, Two Sides

## Operations with Integers

Positive and negative integers are whole numbers that can represent quantities greater than zero and less than zero, respectively.

**Positive Integers:** Positive integers are whole numbers greater than zero. They are denoted by the numbers 1,2,3,4...

**Negative Integers:** Negative integers are whole numbers less than zero. They are denoted by placing a negative sign ("-") before the numbers, such as $-1,-2,-3,-4,...$

The positive integers are used to represent the number of objects, scores, etc. whereas the negative integers can be used to represent debt, losses, temperatures below freezing points, etc.

**Let's solve some problems:**

$$\textbf{1. } 6 - (-8) - 9$$

- Start by simplifying within the parentheses:

$$-(-8) \text{ becomes } 8.$$

- Rewrite the expression with the simplified part:

$$6 + 8 - 9.$$

- Now perform addition and subtraction from left to right:

$$6 + 8 = 14, \text{ then } 14 - 9 = 5$$

$$\textbf{2. } (-5) - (-3) + 10$$

$$(-5) + 3 + 10$$

$$(-5) + 3 = -2, \text{ then } -2 + 10 = 8$$

# Summer Algebra Workbook

## Building Activities

**Operations with Integers**

Evaluate Expressions.

**1)** $(-7) - (-9) =$

**2)** $5 + 10 - 5 =$

**3)** $(-10) - (-4) =$

**4)** $7 - 10 - 2 =$

**5)** $3 - (-9) - 4 =$

**6)** $(-2) + 7 =$

**7)** $(-5) - (-3) + 6 =$

**8)** $(-3) + (-3) - 1 =$

**9)** $10 - 4 + 7 =$

**10)** $(-9) - 3 =$

**11)** $(-7) - (-10) - (-6) =$

**12)** $(-4) + (-1) + 8 =$

**13)** $(-8) - (-4) - (-3) =$

**14)** $8 - (-4) =$

**15)** $(-6) - (-3) =$

**16)** $6 - 8 + 7 =$

**17)** $8 + 5 - 6 =$

**18)** $1 - (-10) =$

**19)** $6 - (-8) - 6 =$

**20)** $7 + (-3) =$

**21)** $(-8) - (-8) + 7 =$

**22)** $8 - (-5) - 8 =$

**23)** $2 + (-2) =$

**24)** $3 - (-5) - 2 =$

**25)** $6 + (-1) - 6 =$

**26)** $(-1) + (-10) + 10 =$

**27)** $10 - 2 - 7 =$

**28)** $4 - (-7) =$

# Order of Operations (PEMDAS)

The order of operations, often remembered by the acronym PEMDAS, stands for:

- **Parentheses**: Perform operations inside parentheses first.
- **Exponents**: Evaluate exponents (powers and roots) next.
- **Multiplication and Division**: Perform multiplication and division from left to right.
- **Addition and Subtraction:** Perform addition and subtraction from left to right.

The order of operations helps to clarify which operations should be performed first in a mathematical expression to ensure consistent and accurate results.

- **Parentheses**: Evaluate expressions within parentheses first. If there are nested parentheses, start with the innermost ones and work your way out.

    1. Example: $2 \times ( 3 + 4) = 2 \times 7 = 14$

- **Exponents**: Evaluate expressions with exponents (powers and roots) next.

    1. Example: $2^3 + 4 = 8 + 4 = 12$

- **Multiplication and Division**: Perform multiplication and division from left to right.

    1. Example: $2 \times 3 + 4 = 6 + 4 = 10$

    2. Example: $6 \div 2 \times 3 = 3 \times 3 = 9$

- **Addition and Subtraction**: Perform addition and subtraction from left to right.

    1. Example: $2 + 3 \times 4 = 2 + 12 = 14$

    2. Example: $10 - 4 \div 2 = 10 - 2 = 8$

## Order of Operations (PEMDAS)

**1)** $(4 + 10)^2 + (10 + 1)^2 =$

**2)** $3 \times (3 + 6) =$

**3)** $6 + 7^2 + 4 + 8^2 =$

**4)** $(2 + 2)^2 + (1 + 9)^2 =$

**5)** $(2 + 6) \div 1 =$

**6)** $3 + 4 - 7 + 7 =$

**7)** $3 + 3 + 4 + 3 =$

**8)** $10 \times (1 + 5) =$

**9)** $2 \times 8 \times 4 =$

**10)** $5 + 5 + 7 + 8 =$

11) $10 + 9 + 8 =$

12) $5 \times 1 =$

13) $(7^2) \times (10^2) + 2 =$

14) $4(3 + 2) =$

15) $5 + 4 - 3 + 4 =$

16) $(10 + 8)^2 + (4 + 2)^2 =$

17) $(8 + 8)^2 + (8 + 8)^2 =$

18) $10 + 4^2 + 6 + 2^2 =$

19) $(5 \times 7) - (5 + 8) =$

20) $8 \times (5 + 1) =$

**21)** $3 + 8 + 4 =$

**22)** $(8^2) \times (3^2) + 1 =$

**23)** $7 + 2^2 =$

**24)** $(9 + 2)^2 =$

**25)** $(2 + 5) \times (7 + 3) =$

**26)** $(8 + 8)(6 + 1) =$

**27)** $4 + 9 + 1 + 2 =$

**28)** $2 + 9 + 2 =$

**29)** $6 + 6 + 5 =$

**30)** $(5 \times 10) - (5 + 4) =$

## Solving One-Step Equations

Solving one-step equations involves finding the value of the variable that makes the equation true. In a one-step equation, there is only one operation (addition, subtraction, multiplication, or division) performed on the variable.

The goal is to isolate the variable on one side of the equation by performing inverse operations.

## For example:

Given the equation $6 = -3z$, where we want to solve for z.

The given equation is already in the form of a one-step equation, with z being multiplied by $-3$.

To isolate z, we need to perform the inverse operation of multiplication, which is division.

Divide both sides by $-3$:

$$\frac{6}{-3} = \frac{-3z}{-3}$$

Simplify:

$$-2 = z$$

So, the solution to the equation is $z = -2$.

When we substitute the value of $z = -2$ back into the original equation, $6 = -3(-2)$, it simplifies to $6 = 6$. This confirms that our solution is correct because it satisfies the original equation.

## Solving One-Step Equations

Solve for the variable.

**1)** $42 = a \cdot 6 + 6$

**2)** $1.3 = 8 \div y$

**3)** $3 \cdot a + a = 28$

**4)** $10 \cdot (m - 8) = -10$

**5)** $-5 = z \cdot (4 - z)$

**6)** $8 = 3x + 2$

**7)** $5z + 2 = 7$

**8)** $28 = 8m - 4$

**9)** $9 = 6z + 3$

**10)** $-8 = b \cdot (7 - b)$

**11)** $56 = a + (a \cdot 6)$

**12)** $(x \div 9) + x = 1.1$

**13)** $60 = (x \cdot 5) + x$

**14)** $s + (s \cdot 9) = 30$

**15)** $3 = a + (a \cdot 2)$

**16)** $k + (4 \div k) = 6.7$

**17)** $7 \cdot x + 10 = 73$

**18)** $y + (10 \div y) = 11$

**19)** $1 + (4 \cdot a) = 21$

**20)** $7 \cdot (k - 9) = -14$

**21)** $25 = b \cdot 7 - 3$

**22)** $(y \div 9) + y = 10$

**23)** $9 = z + 3$

**24)** $1 + 10y = 61$

<u>**Solving Two-Step Equations**</u>

Solving two-step equations involves finding the value of the variable that makes the equation true. In a two-step equation, two operations (addition, subtraction, multiplication, or division) are performed on the variable.

The goal is to isolate the variable on one side of the equation by performing inverse operations in the reverse order of operations.

**For example:**

Given the equation $18 = (10 + b) - 2$, where we want to solve for b.

To solve for b, we need to undo the operations that have been performed on b.

1.  Undo the subtraction by adding 2 to both sides:

$$18 + 2 = (10 + b) - 2 + 2$$
$$20 = 10 + b$$

2. Undo the addition by subtracting 10 from both sides:

$$20 - 10 = 10 + b - 10$$
$$10 = b$$

So, the solution to the equation is $b = 10$

Let's substitute $b = 10$ back into the original equation to verify if it satisfies the equation:

Original equation:

$$18 = (10 + b) - 2:$$

Substitute $b = 10$:

$$18 = (10 + 10) - 2$$

simplify:

$$18 = 20 - 2$$
$$18 = 18$$

Since the equation simplifies to $18 = 18$, it confirms that our solution $b = 10$ is correct.

## Solving Two-Step Equations

Solve for the variable.

**1)** $(6z)^1 = 54$

**2)** $112 = a(6 + a)$

**3)** $10a + 2 = 42$

**4)** $51 = y + 3 + (6y - 8)$

**5)** $-58 = 2 - (10 \cdot b)$

**6)** $112 = 8 \cdot (9 + z)$

**7)** $50 = (10m)^1$

**8)** $10 = y(9 + y)$

9) $z + 8 + 7z = 72$

10) $5 \cdot y - 7 = 28$

11) $46 = 8a + 8a - 2$

12) $8 = a^1 + a - 8$

13) $8 \cdot z - 2 = 78$

14) $y^1 + y - 5 = 15$

15) $56 = 8 \cdot (5 + b)$

16) $s(4 + s) = 96$

**17)** $21 = (9 \cdot m) + 3$

**18)** $8a + 2 + (8a - 1) = 129$

**19)** $24 = (4 - a) \cdot 8$

**20)** $17 = (8 \cdot x) + 1$

**21)** $9b + 7b = 80$

**22)** $37 = 6k + 6 + (6k - 5)$

**23)** $48 = 10s + 2s$

**24)** $-64 = 6 - (7 \cdot a)$

<u>**Solving Multi-Step Equations**</u>

Solving multi-step equations involves finding the value of the variable that makes the equation true. In a multi-step equation, multiple operations (addition, subtraction, multiplication, or division) are performed on the variable.

The goal is to isolate the variable on one side of the equation by performing inverse operations in the reverse order of operations.

**Example:**

Given the equation $-3m - m = -8$, where we want to solve for $m$.

To solve for $m$, we need to undo the operations that have been performed on $m$.

**1.** Combine like terms on the left side:

$$-3m - m = -4m$$

**2.** Substitute the combined term back into the equation:

$$-4m = -8$$

**3.** Undo the multiplication by dividing both sides by $-4-4$:

$$\frac{-4m}{-4} = \frac{-8}{-4}$$

$$m = 2$$

Let's substitute $m = 2$ back into the original equation to verify if it satisfies the equation:

Original equation:

$$-3m - m = -8$$

Substitute $m = 2$:

$$-3(2) - 2 = -8$$

simplify:

$$-6 - 2 = -8$$

$$-8 = -8$$

Since the equation simplifies to $8 = 8$, it confirms that our solution $m = 2$ is correct.

## Solving Multi-Step Equations

Solve for the variable.

**1)** $5(z + 7) + (2z - 4) = 80$

**2)** $10 + k(8 - k) + 7k = 60$

**3)** $(4x + 4)(2x - 9) = -20$

**4)** $8(10 + a) + 5a - 4 = 154$

**5)** $191 = (10k + 1) + (10k - 10)$

**6)** $8 + (x - 3)(7x) = 288$

**7)** $(x + 4) + (9x + 4) = 18$

**8)** $(6k + 10) \cdot (k - 7) = -80$

9) $2z + 9 \cdot (z - 7) = 25$

10) $28 = 1(b - 8) + 8b$

11) $192 = 8(z + 8) + 8z$

12) $4 + (8x + 4) - 3 + (6x) = 131$

**13)** $5m + 7 \cdot (m + 5) = 131$

**14)** $(7 \cdot x) + 3x - 8 = 72$

**15)** $109 = 6k + 5 \cdot (k + 1) - 6$

**16)** $4 + k(4 - k) + 4k = 4$

**17)** $33 = (7 - z) \cdot (4z + 9)$

**18)** $(8 + x)(3x - 1) = 88$

**19)** $10m + 10(m - 8) = 40$

**20)** $(4s + 6) \cdot (s + 1) = 210$

# Solving Equations (One Side)

Solving one-step equations involves performing a single operation to isolate the variable and find its value.

Let's solve an equation step by step: $16 + x = 31$

1. Identify the Goal:

   The goal is to isolate the variable $x$ on one side of the equation.

2. Simplify the Equation: Combine like terms on both sides of the equation, if necessary.

   The equation is already simplified.

3. Undo Addition or Subtraction: If there's addition or subtraction involving the variable, undo it by performing the opposite operation on both sides of the equation.

   Since $x$ is being added to 16, we'll undo this operation by subtracting 16 from both sides of the equation:
   $$16 + x - 16 = 31 - 16$$

4. Isolate the Variable: Ensure that the variable is alone on one side of the equation.

$$x = 15$$

5. Check Your Solution: Substitute the value of $x$ back into the original equation to verify that it satisfies the equation.

$$16 + 15 = 31$$

$$31 = 31$$

The equation is balanced.

## Equations: (One Side)

Solve the equations for the variable.

**1)** $19 \times x = 114$

**2)** $16 \times z = -16$

**3)** $k \div 16 = 13$

**4)** $k \div 10 = -8$

**5)** $m \times 13 = 104$

**6)** $17 + 1y = 9$

**7)** $-2 \times z = -8$

**8)** $z \times -10 = -80$

**9)** $4x - 14 = 2$

**10)** $-110 \div m = 11$

**11)** $z + 16 = 7$

**12)** $y \div 1 = -4$

**13)** $19 - m = 15$

**14)** $6m - 1 = 107$

**15)** $5 - y = 11$

**16)** $m \times 9 = -9$

**17)** $k \div -8 = -7$

**18)** $m \div -8 = -9$

**19)** $11k - -10 = 10$

**20)** $8 - k = 14$

**21)** $-3 + z = 11$

**22)** $17 + m = 36$

**23)** $17 - k = 24$

**24)** $m \div 14 = -4$

## Equations (Two Sides)

A two-sided equation is an equation where both sides have expressions with variables and constants. The goal when solving a two-sided equation is to find the value of the variable that makes both sides equal.

For example: Let's solve an equation:

$$9 + 8x + 8 = 64 + x + 2$$

- Combine Like Terms: Simplify each side of the equation by combining like terms (terms with the same variable or constants).

$$9 + 8x + 8 = 64 + x + 2$$
$$17 + 8x = 66 + x$$

- Isolate the Variable: Use inverse operations to isolate the variable on one side of the equation.

subtract $x$ from both sides:
$$17 + 8x - x = 66 + x - x$$
$$17 + 7x = 66$$

subtracting 17 from both sides:
$$17 - 17 + 7x = 66 - 17$$
$$7x = 49$$

divide both sides by 7:
$$\frac{7x}{7} = \frac{49}{7} = x = 7$$

- Check Solution: Once you find the solution, substitute it back into the original equation to ensure it makes the equation true.

Substitute $x = 7$ back into the original equation:
$$9 + 8(7) + 8 = 64 + 7 + 2$$
$$9 + 56 + 8 = 64 + 7 + 2$$
$$73 = 73$$

## Equations (Two Sides)

Solve for the variable.

**1)**  $9a = -24 + a$

**2)**  $-7 + m = 9 + -7m$

**3)**  $31 + b = 10 + -6b$

**4)**  $64 + y = 9 + -7y + 7$

**5)** $14 + y = 3y$

**6)** $-64 + y = -5 + -10y + 7$

**7)** $6b = -10 + b$

**8)** $7s + 3 = 6s + 9$

**9)** $27 - z + 16 = 9 + 3z + 6$

**10)** $-82 + a = -8a + 8$

**11)** $45 - a = 8a$

**12)** $25 - b = -6b$

**13)** $-45 + x = -4x$

**14)** $-10 + -5z + -1 = -51 - z$

**15)** $-6 - s = -3s$

**16)** $-3m = -20 + m$

17) $-15 + z = -6 + 3z + 5$

18) $-6 + z = 3z$

19) $-3m = -36 + m$

20) $2m = -2 + m$

**21)**  $-7m + -1 = -57 + m$

**22)**  $-48 + s = -7s$

**23)**  $100 - 7s = -2 + 10s$

**24)**  $6 + -3b = 34 + b$

**25)**   $-8 + 3k + 5 = 13 + k + -2$

**26)**   $8a + 0 = 9a + -4$

**27)**   $-6 + 1m = -3 - -4m$

**28)**   $-1 + -9b + -3 = -10 + b + -4$

**29)** $-8 + -3z = -10 + -4z$

**30)** $7 + k = -7 + 8k$

**31)** $1 + 6z + -7 = -1 + z + 0$

**32)** $-10 + 8s = 32 + s$

<u>Simplifying Expressions</u>

It involves combining like terms and performing operations to make the expression easier to understand and work with.

Let's simplify the expression:

$$2x - 2x + 8 + 4$$

- Combine like terms: First, we look for terms with the same variable and exponent. In this expression, $2x$ and $-2x$ are like terms, so they can be combined:

$$2x - 2x = 0$$

- Substitute the simplified terms: After combining the like terms, the expression becomes:

$$0 + 8 + 4$$

- Combine the remaining terms: Now, we add the constants together:

$$8 + 4 = 12$$

# Simplify Expressions

**1)** $3 + 11m - 7m$

**2)** $-10z + 16 - 6z$

**3)** $12y - 1 - 5y + 16$

**4)** $17 + 8m + 16 + 18m$

**5)** $-17 + 18m - 18m - 5 - 16m$

**6)** $9k + 10 - 13 - 5k + 11k$

**7)** $-8m - 13 - 2m$

**8)** $13x + 11 - 18 - 3x + 5x$

**9)** $-6 - 16k + 11 - 10k$

**10)** $14k + 3 + 13k$

**11)** $x - x + 10x + 4 + 16$

**12)** $y - 5y + 6y + 2 + 19$

**13)** $13y + 3 - 2y + 2 + 8y + 14$

**14)** $-12m - 4 + 2m$

**15)** $-10z - 15z$

**16)** $-12 + 13k - 8k - 14 + 7k$

**17)**  $-15m - 7 + m$

**18)**  $-x + 10x$

**19)**  $-y + 5y$

**20)**  $18z - z$

**21)**  $-9y + 9 + 20y$

**22)**  $11z - 3z + 14 + 9$

**23)**  $-4 + 16 - 2m + 20m - 12 + 2m$

**24)**  $-3 - 15m + 3m - 20 + 17m$

**25)** $12 + 16(-5z + 6)$

**26)** $3z + z$

**27)** $12m - 9m + 15 + 1$

**28)** $16k + 1 - 19k + 4 + 20k + 10$

**29)** $-16y + 11 - 11y$

**30)** $13 - 18(-8m + 12)$

**31)** $-8 + 5k - 15k - 14 + 12k$

**32)** $9 + 14m - 19m + 7 - 20m$

<u>**Evaluating Equations**</u>

Evaluating expressions involves substituting given values for variables in an expression and then performing the indicated operations to find the result.

For example: Let's evaluate  $4x - 10$, when $x = 3$:

Step 1: Substitute the given value for the variable:

Replace every occurrence of x in the expression $4x - 10$ with the given value, which is 3:

$$= 4(3) - 10$$

## Step 2: Perform the operations:

Perform the indicated operations according to the order of operations (PEMDAS - Parentheses, Exponents, Multiplication and Division, Addition and Subtraction):

$$= 4 \times 3 - 10$$

Step 3: Simplify:

Calculate the result:

$$12 - 10 = 2$$

## Evaluating Equations

Simplify the following equations when the value of $n = -7$

**1)** $9 \cdot (1 - n) =$

**2)** $n(-7 + n) =$

**3)** $(3n)^2 =$

**4)** $n \div 10 =$

**5)** $-9 + (n - -1)(4n) =$

**6)** $n + (-2 \div n) =$

**7)** $-1 + (n - -7) =$

**8)** $-5 + -2n - n(-4 + n) =$

## Evaluating Equations

Simplify the following equations when the value of $n = 2$

**1)** $10n + -4n + 10n =$

**2)** $(-7 - n) \cdot 5 =$

**3)** $5 + (-6n + -10) =$

**4)** $n^3 + n - -4 =$

**5)** $n \cdot 8 + 5 =$

**6)** $(6 - n) \cdot (-4n + -10) =$

**7)** $2n + 8 =$

**8)** $9(n + 8) + (-1n - -6) =$

## Evaluating Equations

Simplify the following equations when the value of $n = 2$

**1)** $8n + -10(n + -7) - n =$

**2)** $n + -10 =$

**3)** $7n^2 + -6n^1 =$

**4)** $n \cdot (-3 - n) =$

**5)** $n + (10 \div n) =$

**6)** $8 + 5n =$

**7)** $n^2 + n - 10 =$

**8)** $-6 \cdot n + n =$

## Evaluating Equations

Simplify the following equations when the value of  n = 1

**1)**  n + -2 + 8n =

**2)**  n + (4 · n) – 6 =

**3)**  10 · n + n =

**4)**  -4(n – 5) + 10n =

**5)**  4n + -5n =

**6)**  n · 7 =

**7)**  -3 + (-2 · n) =

**8)**  8n + (1 · n) – 5 =

## Verbal Algebra Expressions

Verbal algebra involves translating word problems or verbal statements into algebraic expressions or equations.

For example: The product of the two numbers is 91. One number is six less than the other. What are the numbers?

We're given a verbal description of a problem, and we need to represent it using algebraic symbols and equations.

Let's break down the given problem into algebraic expressions:

- Given that the product of the two numbers is 91, we can write the equation: $xy = 91$
- Also, given that one number is six less than the other, we can write another equation: $x = y - 6$

Now, we can use algebraic techniques to solve the system of equations to find the values of $x$ and $y$, which represent the two numbers.

$$x (x - 6) = 91$$

1. Solve the equation:

   - Expand the equation:

   $$x^2 - 6x = 91$$

   - Rearrange the equation into standard quadratic form:

   $$x^2 - 6x - 91 = 0$$

   - Factor the quadratic equation:

   $$(x - 13) (x + 7) = 0$$

2. Find the solutions for $x$:

   - From the factored form, we have two possible values for $x$:

$$x = 13 \text{ or } x = -7$$

3. Check the validity of the solutions:

- Since one number is six less than the other, we discard the negative solution.

- Therefore, the solution is $x = 13$.

4. Find the other number:

- Substitute $x = 13$ into the expression for the other number:

Other number $= x - 6 = 13 - 6 = 7$

So, the two numbers are 13 and 7.

## Verbal Algebra Expressions

**1)** One-half of a number increased by 7 is 15. What is the number?

**2)** The sum of a number and three is 4. Find the number.

**3)** The product of six and some number is equal to the sum of that number and 20. What is the number?

**4)** The sum of two consecutive numbers is 3. What are the numbers?

**5)**      Eight times a number is 0. What is the number?

**6)**      The sum of the first and third of three consecutive numbers is 16. Find the numbers.

**7)**      Three is equal to the quotient of a number and 7. Find the number.

**8)**      The quotient of a number and five is 7. Find the number.

**9)** Three times a number equals 18 less than five times the number. What is the number?

**10)** Six more than a number is 13. What is the number?

**11)** The sum of four consecutive even numbers is 20. What are the numbers?

**12)** The sum of the largest and eight times the smallest of three consecutive numbers is equal to 56. Find the numbers.

**13)** Find two consecutive even integers such that seven times the smaller decreased by the larger is 22.

**14)** The difference of two numbers is 61. The larger number is 7 more than ten times the smaller number. What are the numbers?

**15)** The product of eight and some number is equal to the sum of that number and 42. What is the number?

**16)** The difference of two numbers is 44. The larger number is 8 more than ten times the smaller number. What are the numbers?

**17)** 49 is equal to the product of seven and some number. Find the number.

**18)** The quotient of a number and nine increased by 4 is 12. What is the number?

**19)** The quotient of a number and five is 7. Find the number.

**20)** One number is 12 more than another number. The sum of nine times the larger number and four times the smaller is 121. What are the numbers?

# Solving Inequalities

Inequalities are mathematical expressions that compare the relative sizes of two values. They are used to express relationships where one quantity is:

- "$<$" (less than),
- "$>$" (greater than),
- "$<=$" (less than or equal to),
- "$>=$" (greater than or equal to),
- and "$\neq$" (not equal to) another quantity.

For example:

$$y + \text{-}10 \leq -8$$

To isolate $y$, we need to get rid of the constant term $-10$. Since $-10$ is being subtracted from $y$, we can undo this operation by adding 10 to both sides of the inequality:

$$y - 10 + 10 \leq -8 + 10$$

$$y \leq 2$$

To check the solution:

$$2 - 10 \leq -8$$

$$-8 = -8$$

The inequality is true when $y = 2$

## Solving Inequalities

1) $$\frac{k}{6} \le -6$$

2) $$-7 + k < -2$$

3) $$-7 - a \le 3$$

4) $$5s > 6$$

**5)**

$k - -1 < 1$

**6)**

$14\,m > -6$

**7)**

$\dfrac{a}{-6} < 7$

**8)**

$y + -3 > -9$

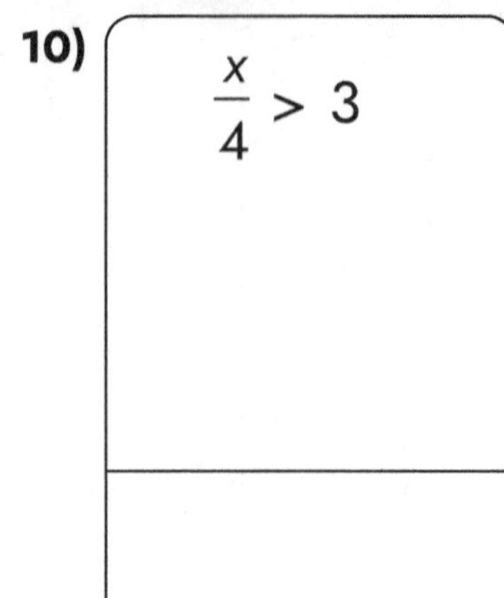

**9)** $m - -7 \leq 7$

**10)** $\dfrac{x}{4} > 3$

**11)** $4 + b \leq -9$

**12)** $-8\,m > -10$

13)
$$\frac{b}{-4} < 4$$

14)
$$b - -4 \leq 9$$

15)
$$-3 + s \geq -2$$

16)
$$-6\,a > -15$$

17)
$$3 + b \leq -8$$

18)
$$s - -5 \geq -2$$

19)
$$\frac{k}{-4} \geq -8$$

20)
$$4a \leq 10$$

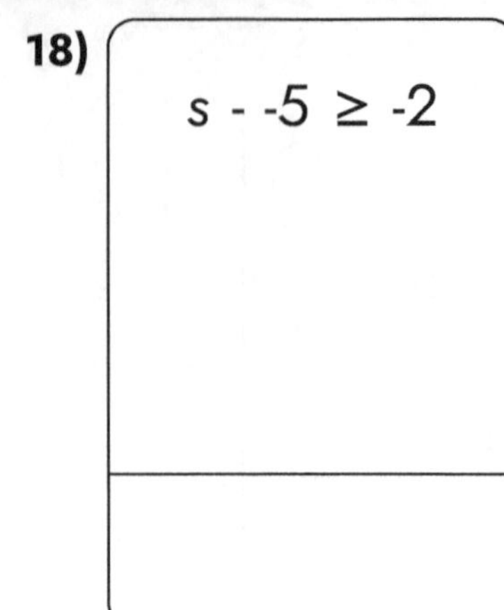

## Linear Functions

A linear equation is an algebraic equation that represents a straight line when graphed on a coordinate plane. It consists of variables raised to the power of 1 (i.e., no exponents higher than 1) and constant coefficients.

The general form of a linear equation in one variable x is:

$$ax + b = 0$$

Where $a$ and $b$ are constants, and $x$ is the variable.

Let's solve the linear equation:

$$-2x + 9 = 5$$

- **Isolate the variable term:** We want to isolate the term containing $x$ on one side of the equation. To do this, we'll move the constant term to the other side. Subtract 9 from both sides:

$$-2x + 9 - 9 = 5 - 9$$

$$-2x = -4$$

- **Divide by the coefficient of the variable:** To solve for $x$, divide both sides by the coefficient of $x$, which is -2:

$$\frac{-2x}{-2} = \frac{-4}{-2}$$

$$x = 2$$

## Linear Equations

Solve for the variable.

**1)** $2x = 10$

**2)** $1(-5x - (-3)) = 38$

**3)** $8y + (-1)y - 6 = 50$

**4)** $-10x + 3x = 7$

**5)** $8x - 8 = 8$

**6)** $2x + (-6)x - (-8) = 16$

**7)** $-6x + (-5)x - (-8) = 96$

**8)** $-6x + (-8)x - (-7) = 105$

9) $3x + 7 = -8$

10) $-8y + 9 = -63$

11) $8y + 2 = 82$

12) $8(-1x - 1) = 24$

13) $7x = -63$

14) $2y - 7 = 3$

15) $4x = 20$

16) $5y = -10$

**17)** $x + 10x - (-1) = 100$

**18)** $10y = -10$

**19)** $-1x - (-10) = 12$

**20)** $10x + 5x - (-6) = -84$

**21)** $-6y = -54$

**22)** $8y + 5 = 13$

**23)** $-10(2y - 4) = 140$

**24)** $9y + 1 = 82$

<u>**Slop from Two Points**</u>

The slope between two points on a Cartesian coordinate system is a measure of the steepness of the line connecting those points. It's calculated by finding the change in the y-coordinates divided by the change in the x-coordinates.

- The coordinates of the first point as $(x1 , y1) =( 2,-30)$.

- The coordinates of the second point as $(x2 , y2) = (-5,40)$.

The formula to calculate the slope ($m$) between two points:

$$\frac{y2 - y1}{x2 - x1}$$

## Find Slope from two Points

**1)** (-6, 13 ) and (-3 , 1 )

**2)** (19, -19 ) and (7 , 4 )

**3)** (-20, -15 ) and (-2 , 13 )

**4)** (13, 4 ) and (0 , 9 )

**5)** (11, 5 ) and (12 , -12 )

**6)** (-8, -15 ) and (8 , 17 )

**7)** (9, -9 ) and (-7 , -13 )

**8)** (10, 8 ) and (4 , 16 )

**9)** (12, 5 ) and (10 , 14 )

**10)** (-17, 16 ) and (2 , -10 )

**11)** (-12, -19 ) and (-3 , -3 )

**12)** (11, -8 ) and (-19 , 12 )

**13)** (15, -15 ) and (1 , 18 )

**14)** (-6, 15 ) and (5 , -12 )

**15)** (-15, 0 ) and (13 , 8 )

**16)** (9, -1 ) and (15 , -7 )

**17)** (1, 2 ) and (-19 , -12 )

**18)** (14, 6 ) and (6 , 15 )

**19)** (-18, 1 ) and (20 , -10 )

**20)** (9, -10 ) and (-15 , -4 )

**21)** (-11, 1 ) and (-7 , 4 )

**22)** (-14, 7 ) and (2 , 18 )

**23)** (20, 1 ) and (8 , 3 )

**24)** (-17, 15 ) and (1 , 9 )

## Graphing Linear Equation

Graphing a linear equation involves plotting the points that satisfy the equation on a coordinate plane and connecting them to form a straight line. Linear equations are equations of the form $y = mx + b$, where $m$ represents the slope of the line, and $b$ represents the y-intercept, the point where the line intersects the y-axis.

To graph a linear equation:

1. Identify the slope ($m$) and y-intercept ($b$) from the equation.

2. Plot the y-intercept $(0,b)$) as a point on the y-axis.

3. Use the slope to find additional points on the line. The slope represents the change in y for every unit change in x.

4. Connect the points to form a straight line.

For example, to graph the equation:

$$y = \frac{9}{4}x - 8$$

1. **Identify the slope and y-intercept:** The slope is $\frac{9}{4}$, and the y-intercept is −8.

2. **Plot the y-intercept:** Plot the point $(0,-8)$.

3. **Use the slope to plot additional points:** the slop is $\frac{9}{4}$ to find another point. we will move up 9 units and 4 units to the right from the y-intercept to find another point.

4. **Draw the line:** Once we have at least two points, we can draw a straight line.

We can continue this process to plot more points and extend the line further if needed.

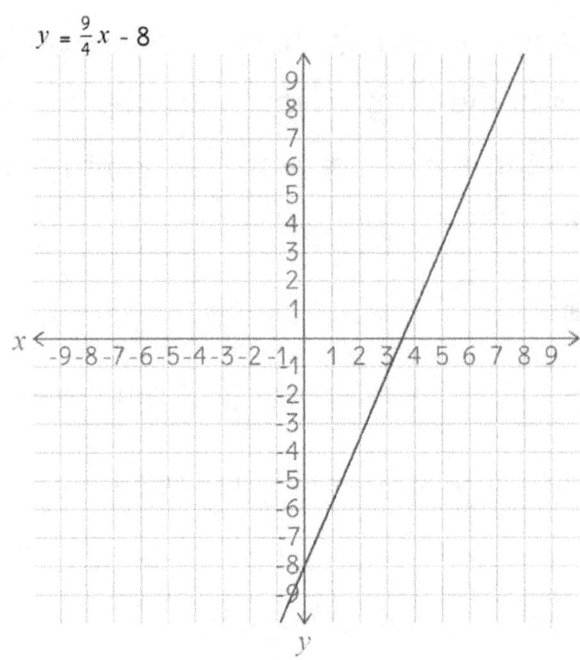

## Graphing Linear Equations

1) $y = \dfrac{1}{2}x + 3$

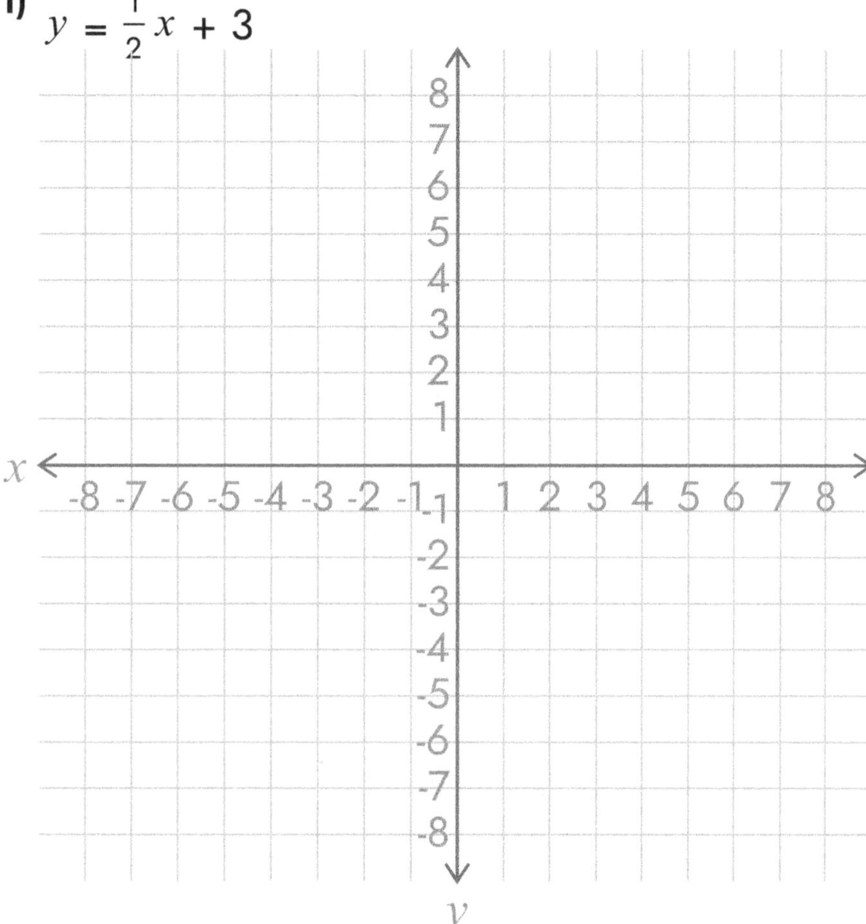

**2)**

$y = -2x - 2$

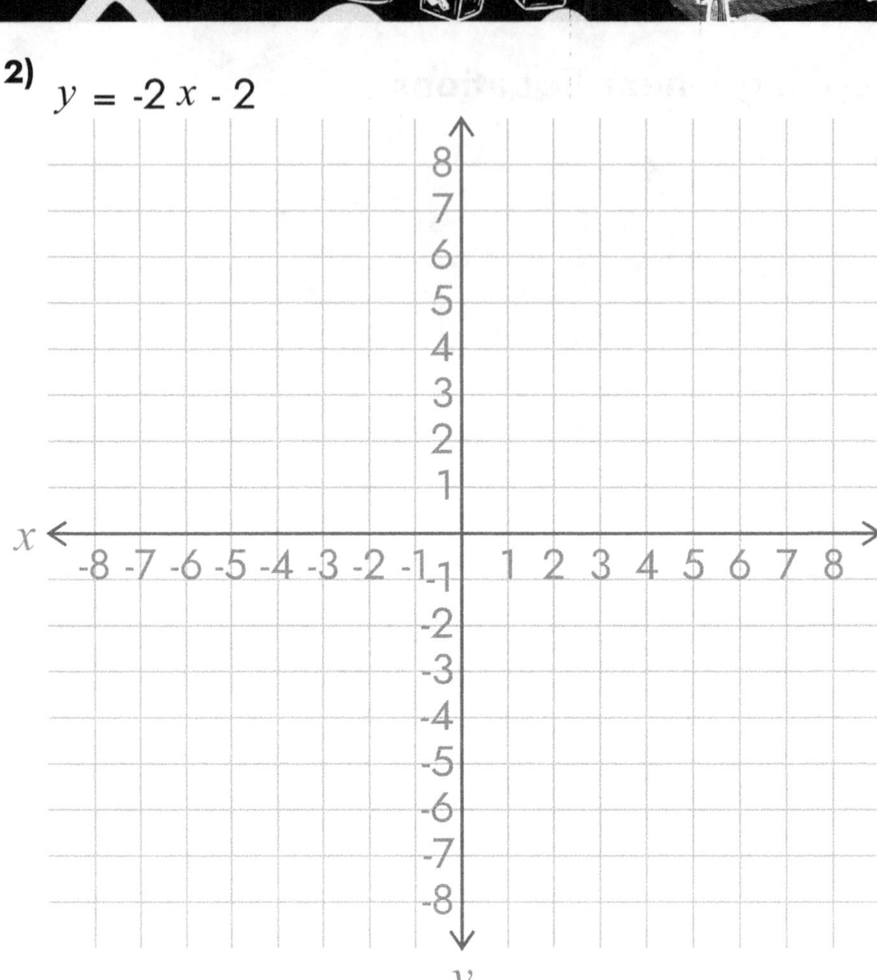

**3)** $y = -x - 2$

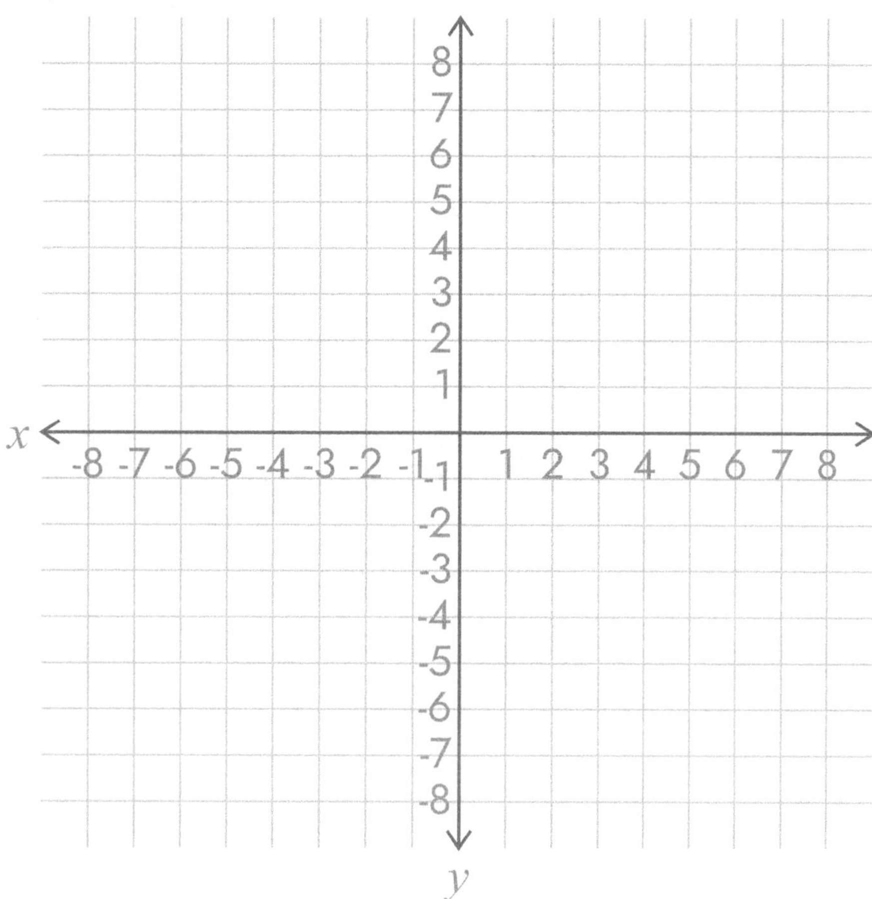

**4)** $y = -3x - 8$

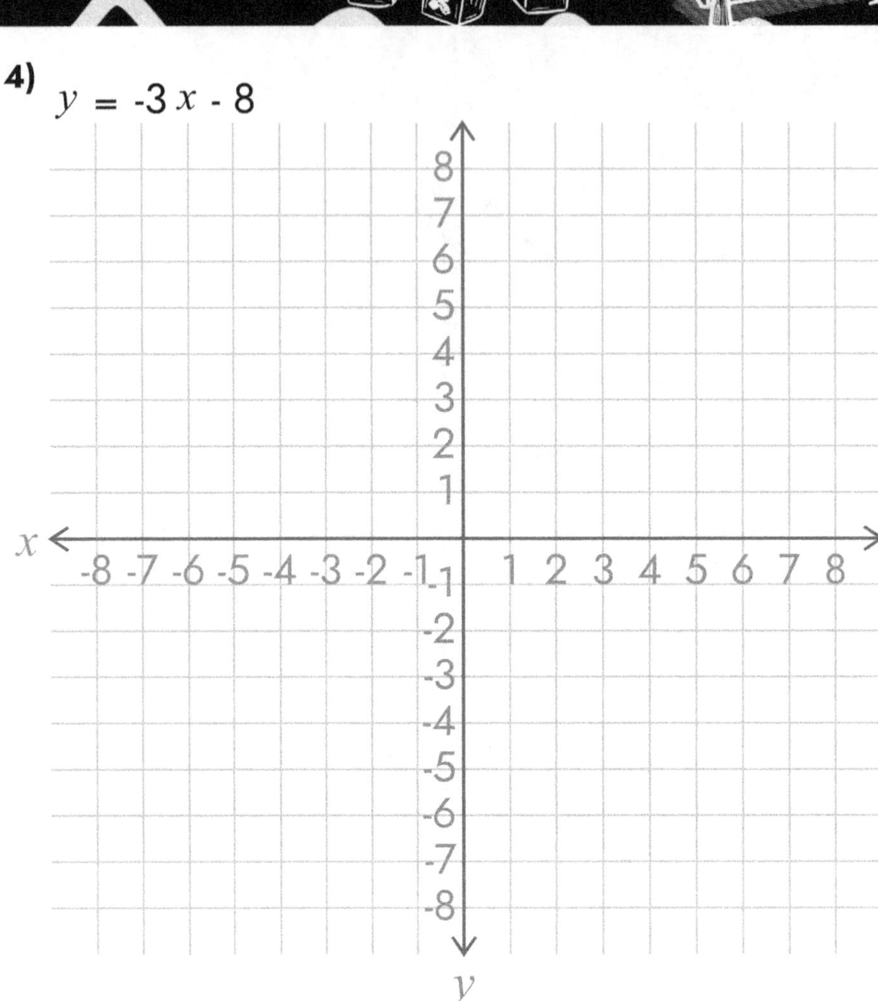

**5)** $y = -x - 4$

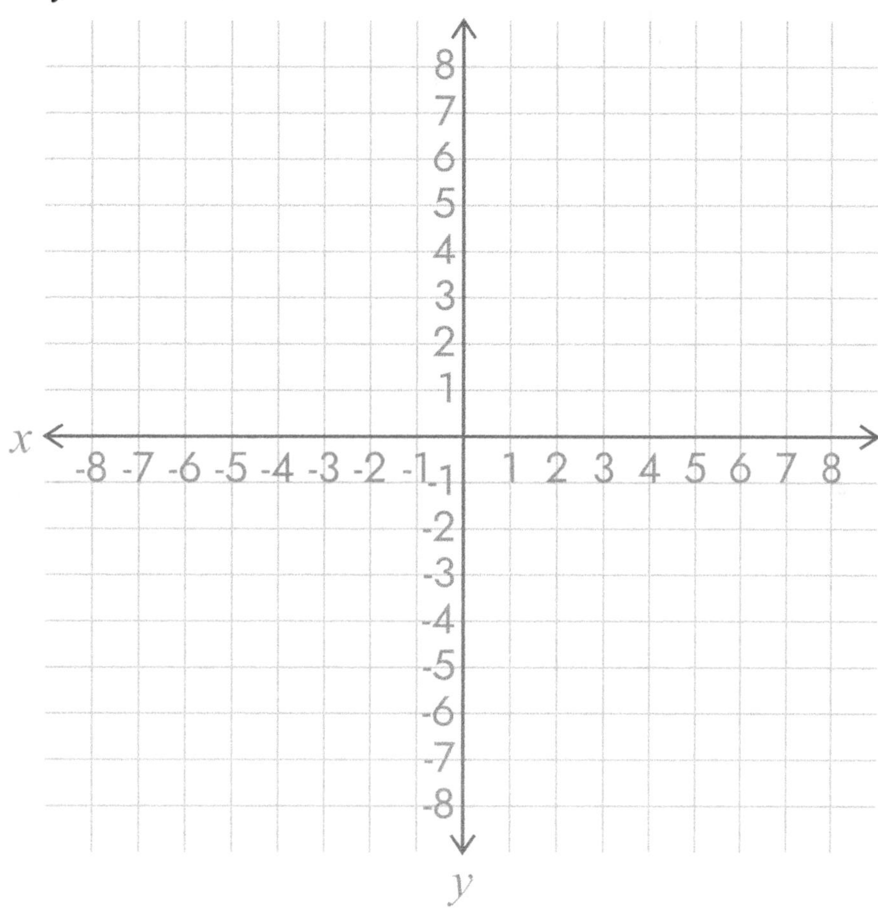

## Plotting Lines

Plot and draw the lines.

**1)**

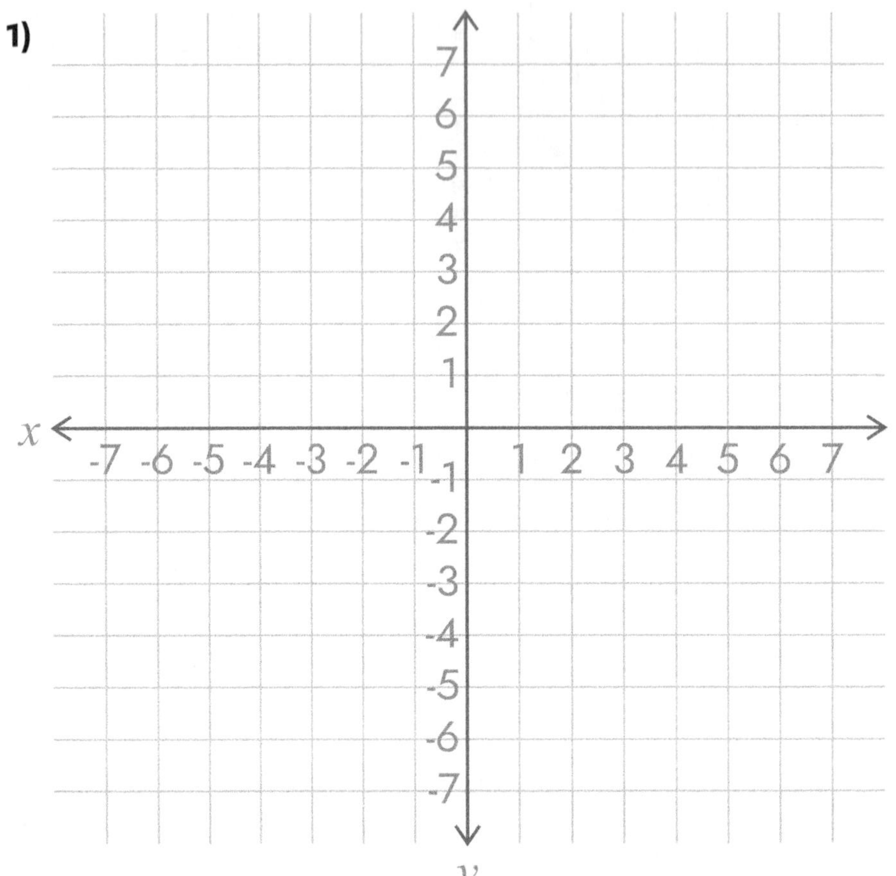

A = (-2, 3)          B = (-6, 1)

C = (2, 5)           D = (-4, 2)

E = (6, 7)           F = (4, 6)

**2)**

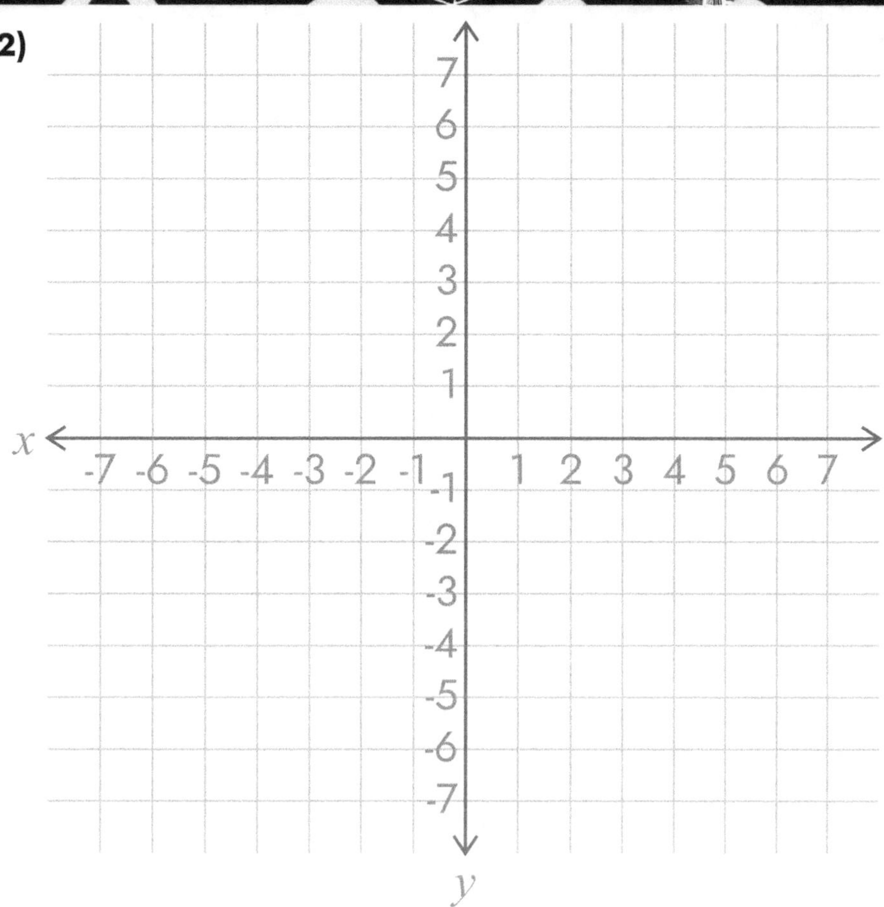

A = (-2, 0)        B = (0, 0)

C = (1, 0)         D = (2, 0)

E = (-1, 0)        F = (3, 0)

**3)**

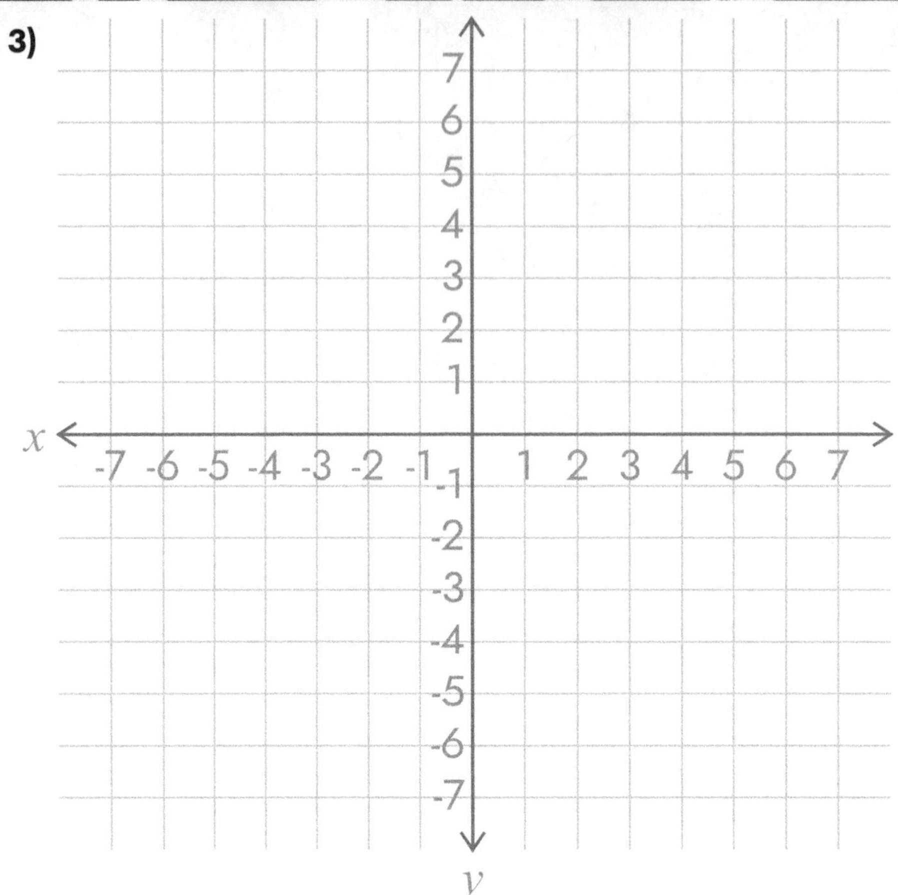

A =  (-2, 4)          B =  (-3, 6)

C =  (0, 0)           D =  (2, -4)

E =  (-1, 2)          F =  (1, -2)

**4)**

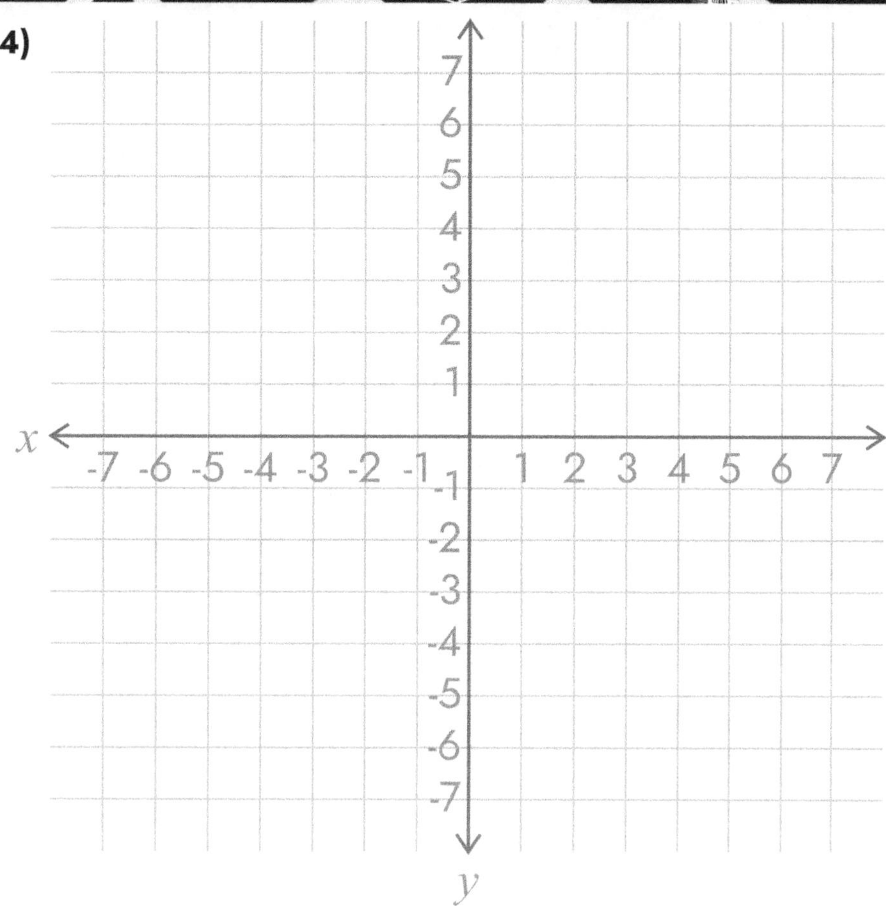



A = (-7, -6)          B = (1, 2)

C = (6, 7)            D = (-3, -2)

E = (4, 5)            F = (-6, -5)

5)

A = (-1, -3)          B = (2, 3)

C = (0, -1)          D = (3, 5)

E = (1, 1)          F = (-2, -5)

## Quadratic Equations

A quadratic equation is a polynomial equation of the second degree, meaning it can be written in the form:

$$ax^2 + bx + c = 0$$

where a, b, and c are constants, and x is the variable being solved for. The solutions to a quadratic equation are the values of x that make the equation true.

Now, let's solve the quadratic equation $11x^2 - 1 = 0$ and understand it step by step using quadratic formula.

1. Identify the coefficients:

   In the equation $11x^2 - 1 = 0$,
   $$a=11, \ b=0, \text{ and } c=-1.$$

2. Apply the quadratic formula:

   The quadratic formula states that for an equation $ax^2 + bx + c = 0$, the solutions for x are given by:
   $$x = \frac{-b \pm \sqrt{b^2 - 4ac}}{2a}$$

   Plugging in the values a=11, b=0, and c=−1 into the quadratic formula, we get:
   $$x = \frac{-0 \pm \sqrt{0 - 4(11)(-1)}}{2(11)}$$

3. Simplify inside the square root:

   $$0^2 - 4(11)\,(-1) = 0 - (-44) = 44$$

4. Plug in the simplified values:
   $$x = \frac{\pm \sqrt{44}}{22}$$

5. Simplify the square root:

   Since 44 is not a perfect square, we can write it as $\sqrt[2]{11}$

$$x = \frac{\pm \sqrt[2]{11}}{22}$$

6. Simplify further if possible:

    We can simplify $\sqrt[2]{11}$ to $\sqrt{11}$ by canceling out the common factor:

$$x = \frac{\pm \sqrt{11}}{11}$$

7. Final solution:

    So, the solutions to the equation are:

$$x = \frac{\sqrt{11}}{11} \text{ and } x = \frac{-\sqrt{11}}{11}$$

$$\text{or}$$

$$(x = 0.302, \text{ and } x = -0.302)$$

These are the roots of the quadratic equation. They represent the points where the graph of the quadratic equation intersects the x-axis.

Let's solve another equation:

$$-4p^2 + 6p - 6 = 0$$

$$p = \frac{-b \pm \sqrt{b^2 - 4ac}}{2a}$$

where $a = -4$, $b = 6$, and $c = -6$.

Let's plug these values into the quadratic formula:

$$p = \frac{-6 \pm \sqrt{6^2 - 4(-4)(-6)}}{2(-4)}$$

First, let's simplify inside the square root:

$$6^2 - 4(-4)(-6)$$

$$= 36 - 96 = -60$$

So, we have:

$$p = \frac{-6 \pm \sqrt{-60}}{-8}$$

We can simplify the square root of $-60$ by factoring out $-1$:

$$\sqrt{-60}$$

$$= \sqrt{-1 \times 60}$$

$$= \sqrt{-1} \times \sqrt{60}$$

$$= i\sqrt{60}$$

So, we have:

$$p = \frac{-6 \pm i\sqrt{60}}{-8}$$

Simplify:

$$\sqrt{60} \text{ to } \sqrt{4 \times 15} = 2\sqrt{15}$$

$$p = \frac{-6 \pm i \times 2\sqrt{15}}{-8}$$

Now, divide both the numerator and denominator by $-2$ to simplify:

$$p = \frac{3 \pm i\sqrt{15}}{4}$$

So, the solutions to the equation are:

$$p = \frac{3 + i\sqrt{15}}{4} \text{ and } p = \frac{3 - i\sqrt{15}}{4}$$

This equation $-4p^2 + 6p - 6 = 0$ has no real solutions.

When a quadratic equation has no real solutions, it means that the solutions are not real numbers, but rather complex numbers. In this case, the solutions involve the imaginary unit $i$ because the discriminant ($b^2 - 4ac$) is negative, which results in taking the square root of a negative number when applying the quadratic formula.

In mathematics, such equations are said to have "no real roots" or "no real solutions." They are also sometimes referred to as having "complex roots" or "complex solutions." Complex numbers include a real part and an imaginary part, and they are often written in the form $a + bi$, where $a$ and $b$ are real numbers and $i$ is the imaginary unit, defined as $i = \sqrt{-1}$.

Let's solve another equation:

$$12x^2 + 6x - 2 = 0$$

$$x = \frac{-b \pm \sqrt{b^2 - 4ac}}{2a}$$

where $a = 12$, $b = 6$, and $c = -2$.

Let's plug these values into the quadratic formula:

$$x = \frac{-6 \pm \sqrt{6^2 - 4(12)(-2)}}{2(12)}$$

First, let's simplify inside the square root:

$$6^2 - 4(12)(-2)$$
$$= 36 - (-96)$$
$$= 36 + 96$$
$$= 132$$

So, we have:

$$x = \frac{-6 \pm \sqrt{132}}{24}$$

Now, let's simplify the square root of 132:

$$x = \frac{-6 \pm \sqrt{4 \times 33}}{24}$$
$$x = \frac{-6 \pm 2\sqrt{33}}{24}$$
$$x = \frac{-6 \pm \sqrt{33}}{12}$$

So, the solutions to the equation are:

$$x = \frac{-6 + \sqrt{33}}{12} \text{ and } x = \frac{-6 - \sqrt{33}}{12}$$

or $(x = 0.229$, and $x = -0.729)$

Let's solve a quadratic equation where the right side is a number, instead of 0.

$$-8n^2 + 6n + 30 = 7$$

To solve the equation, we first need to bring all terms to one side to set the equation equal to zero:

$$-8n^2 + 6n + 30 - 7 = 0$$

Simplify:

$$-8n^2 + 6n + 23 = 0$$

Now, to solve for n, we can use the quadratic formula:

$$n = \frac{-b \pm \sqrt{b^2 - 4ac}}{2a}$$

where $a = -8$, $b = 6$, and $c = 23$.

Plugging these values into the formula, we get:

$$n = \frac{-6 \pm \sqrt{6^2 - 4(-8)(23)}}{2(-8)}$$

$$n = \frac{-6 \pm \sqrt{36 + 736}}{-16}$$

$$n = \frac{-6 \pm \sqrt{772}}{-16}$$

Now, let's simplify the square root of 772. We can factor out 4:

$$\sqrt{772} = \sqrt{4 \times 193} = 2\sqrt{193}$$

So, our equation becomes:

$$n = \frac{-6 \pm 2\sqrt{193}}{-8}$$

So, the solutions to the equation are:

$$n = \frac{-3 + \sqrt{193}}{-8} \text{ and } n = \frac{-3 - \sqrt{193}}{-8}$$

*or*

$$(n = -1.362, \text{ and } n = 2.112)$$

## Quadratic Equations

1. $6n^2 + 3 = 0$

2. $3m^2 - 5m - 2 = 0$

3. $7n^2 - 21 = 0$

4. $5n^2 - 4n - 15 = 0$

5. $-3m^2 + 22 = 0$

6. $2b^2 - 8b - 42 = 0$

**7.** $p^2 - 64 = 0$

**10.** $7k^2 - 10k - 3 = 0$

**8.** $-7x^2 - 3x + 19 = 0$

**11.** $4b^2 - 2b - 60 = 12$

**9.** $12b^2 - 8 = 0$

**12.** $-3p^2 - p + 26 = 2$

**13.** $3x^2 - 5x - 10 = -7$

**16.** $-6r^2 = -3 - 8r$

**14.** $-4n^2 - 3n + 7 = -3$

**17.** $4x^2 - 63 = -9x$

**15.** $11m^2 + 12m - 9 = 6$

**18.** $6v^2 - 13 = -5v$

# ANSWERS

**Page 1:   Operations with Integers**

**1.** 2    **2.** 10    **3.** -6    **4.** -5    **5.** 8    **6.** 5    **7.** 4    **8.** -7    **9.** 13

**10.** -12    **11.** 9    **12.** 3    **13.** -1    **14.** 12    **15.** -3    **16.** 5    **17.** 7    **18.** 11

**19.** 8    **20.** 4    **21.** 7    **22.** 5    **23.** 0    **24.** 6    **25.** -1    **26.** -1    **27.** 1

**28.** 11

**Page 4:   Order of Operations (PEMDAS)**

**1.** 317    **2.** 27    **3.** 123    **4.** 116    **5.** 8    **6.** 7    **7.** 13

**8.** 60    **9.** 64    **10.** 25    **11.** 27    **12.** 5    **13.** 4,902    **14.** 20

**15.** 10    **16.** 360    **17.** 512    **18.** 36    **19.** 22    **20.** 48    **21.** 15

**22.** 577    **23.** 11    **24.** 121    **25.** 70    **26.** 112    **27.** 16    **28.** 13

**29.** 17    **30.** 41

**Page 7:   Solving One-Step Equations**

**1.** 6    **2.** 6    **3.** 7    **4.** 7    **5.** 5 or -1    **6.** 2

**7.** 1    **8.** 4    **9.** 1    **10.** 8 or -1    **11.** 8    **12.** 1

**13.** 10    **14.** 3    **15.** 1    **16.** 6    **17.** 9    **18.** 10 or 1

**19.** 5    **20.** 7    **21.** 4    **22.** 9    **23.** 6    **24.** 6

**Page 10:   Solving Two-Step Equations**

**1.** 9    **2.** 8 or -14    **3.** 4    **4.** 8    **5.** 6    **6.** 5

**7.** 5    **8.** 1 or -10    **9.** 8    **10.** 7    **11.** 3    **12.** 8

**13.** 10    **14.** 10    **15.** 2    **16.** 8 or -12    **17.** 2    **18.** 8

**19.** 1    **20.** 2    **21.** 5    **22.** 3    **23.** 4    **24.** 10

**Page 13:  Solving Multi-Step Equations**

**1.** 7  **2.** 10 or 5  **3.** 4  **4.** 6  **5.** 10  **6.** 8 or -5  **7.** 1

**8.** 5  **9.** 8  **10.** 4  **11.** 8  **12.** 9  **13.** 8  **14.** 8

**15.** 10  **16.** 8 or 0  **17.** 6  **18.** 3  **19.** 6  **20.** 6

**Page 18:  Equations: (One Side)**

**1.** $x = 6$  **2.** $z = -1$  **3.** $k = 208$  **4.** $k = -80$  **5.** $m = 8$  **6.** $y = -8$

**7.** $z = 4$  **8.** $z = 8$  **9.** $x = 4$  **10.** $m = -10$  **11.** $z = -9$  **12.** $y = -4$

**13.** $m = 4$  **14.** $m = 18$  **15.** $y = -6$  **16.** $m = -1$  **17.** $k = 56$  **18.** $m = 72$

**19.** $k = 0$  **20.** $k = -6$  **21.** $z = 14$  **22.** $m = 19$  **23.** $k = -7$  **24.** $m = -56$

**Page 21:  Equations (Two Sides)**

**1.** $a = -3$  **2.** $m = 2$  **3.** $b = -3$  **4.** $y = -6$  **5.** $y = 7$  **6.** $y = 6$

**7.** $b = -2$  **8.** $s = 6$  **9.** $z = 7$  **10.** $a = 10$  **11.** $a = 5$  **12.** $b = -5$

**13.** $x = 9$  **14.** $z = 10$  **15.** $s = 3$  **16.** $m = 5$  **17.** $z = -7$  **18.** $z = -3$

**19.** $m = 9$  **20.** $m = -2$  **21.** $m = 7$  **22.** $s = 6$  **23.** $s = 6$  **24.** $b = -7$

**25.** $k = 7$  **26.** $a = 4$  **27.** $m = -1$  **28.** $b = 1$  **29.** $z = -2$  **30.** $k = 2$

**31.** $z = 1$  **32.** $s = 6$

**Page 29:  Simplify Expressions**

**1.** $4m + 3$  **2.** $-16z + 16$  **3.** $7y + 15$  **4.** $26m + 33$

**5.** $-16m - 22$  **6.** $15k - 3$  **7.** $-10m - 13$  **8.** $15x - 7$

**9.** $-26k + 5$  **10.** $27k + 3$  **11.** $10x + 20$  **12.** $2y + 21$

**13.** $19y + 19$  **14.** $-10m - 4$  **15.** $-25z$  **16.** $12k - 26$

**17.** $-14m - 7$  **18.** $9x$  **19.** $4y$  **20.** $17z$

**21.** 11y + 9     **22.** 8z + 23     **23.** 20m     **24.** 5m – 23

**25.** –80z + 108     **26.** 4z     **27.** 3m + 16     **28.** 17k + 15

**29.** –27y + 11     **30.** 144m – 203     **31.** 2k – 22     **32.** –25m + 16

## Page 33:  Evaluating Equations

**1.** 72    **2.** 98    **3.** 441    **4.** -0.7    **5.** 159    **6.** -6.7    **7.** -1    **8.** -68

## Page 34:  Evaluating Equations

**1.** 32    **2.** -45    **3.** -17    **4.** 14    **5.** 21    **6.** -72    **7.** 12    **8.** 94

## Page 35:  Evaluating Equations

**1.** 64    **2.** -8    **3.** 16    **4.** -10    **5.** 7    **6.** 18    **7.** -4    **8.** -10

## Page 36:  Evaluating Equations

**1.** 7    **2.** -1    **3.** 11    **4.** 26    **5.** -1    **6.** 7    **7.** -5    **8.** 4

## Page 37:  Verbal Algebra Expressions

**1.** 16     **2.** 1     **3.** 4     **4.** 1, 2     **5.** 0

**6.** 7, 8, 9     **7.** 21     **8.** 35     **9.** 9     **10.** 7

**11.** 2, 4, 6, 8     **12.** 6, 7, 8     **13.** 4, 6     **14.** 6, 67     **15.** 6

**16.** 4, 48     **17.** 7     **18.** 72     **19.** 35     **20.** 1, 13

## Page 42:  Solving Inequalities

**1.** $k \le -36$     **2.** $k < 5$     **3.** $a \le -10$     **4.** $s > 6/5$     **5.** $k < 0$

**6.** $m > -3/7$     **7.** $a < -42$     **8.** $y > -6$     **9.** $m \le 0$     **10.** $x > 12$

**11.** $b \le -13$     **12.** $m > 5/4$     **13.** $b < -16$     **14.** $b \le 5$     **15.** $s \ge 1$

**16.** $a > 5/2$     **17.** $b \le -11$     **18.** $s \ge -7$     **19.** $k \ge 32$     **20.** $a \le 5/2$

## Page 47:  Linear Equations

**1.** 5    **2.** -7    **3.** 8    **4.** -1    **5.** 2    **6.** -2    **7.** -8    **8.** -7    **9.** -5    **10.** 9

**11.** 10    **12.** -4    **13.** -9    **14.** 5    **15.** 5    **16.** -2    **17.** 9    **18.** -1    **19.** -2    **20.** -6

**21.** 9    **22.** 1    **23.** -5    **24.** 9

## Page 50: Find Slope from two Points

**1.** -4    **2.** -1.92    **3.** 1.56    **4.** -0.38    **5.** -17    **6.** 2    **7.** 0.25

**8.** -1.33    **9.** -4.5    **10.** -1.37    **11.** 1.78    **12.** -0.67    **13.** -2.36    **14.** -2.45

**15.** 0.29    **16.** -1    **17.** 0.7    **18.** -1.12    **19.** -0.29    **20.** -0.25    **21.** 0.75

**22.** 0.69    **23.** -0.17    **24.** -0.33

## Page 53: Graphing Linear Equations

**1.** 

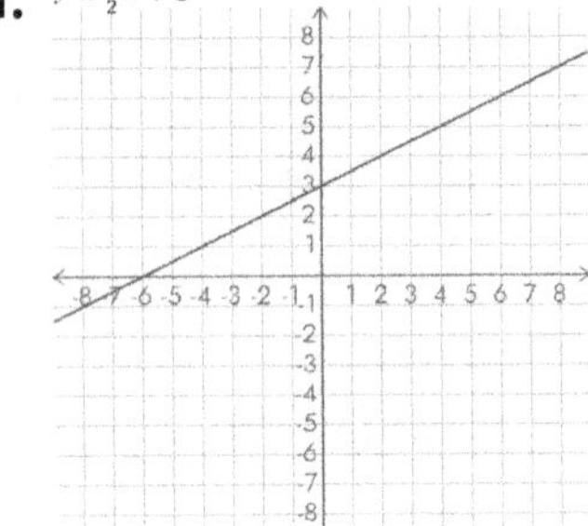

**2.** 

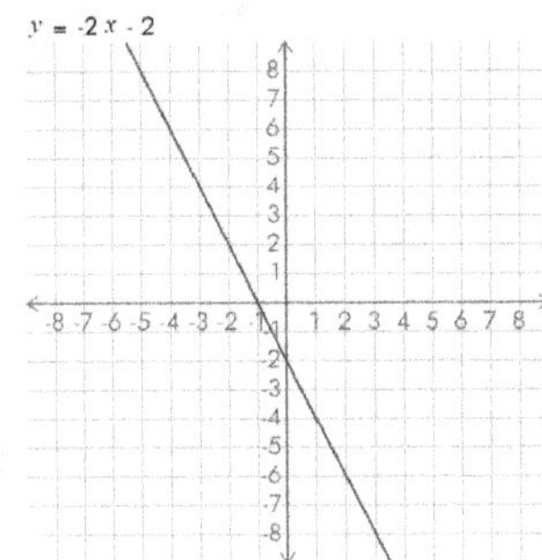

**3.** 

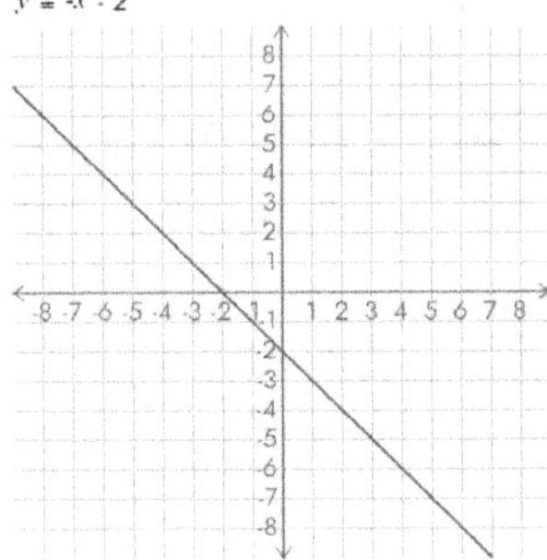

**4.** 

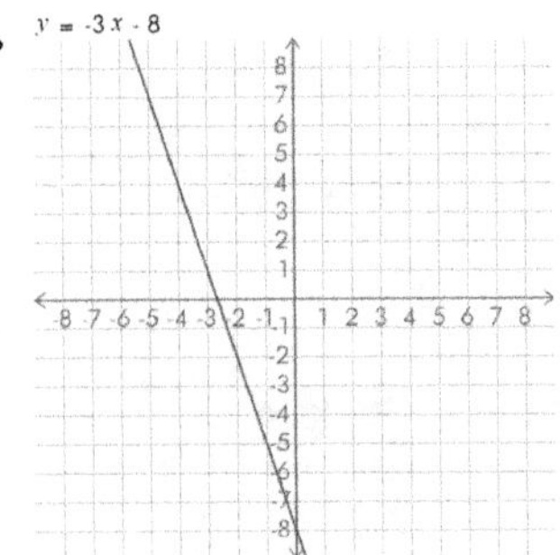

**5.** 

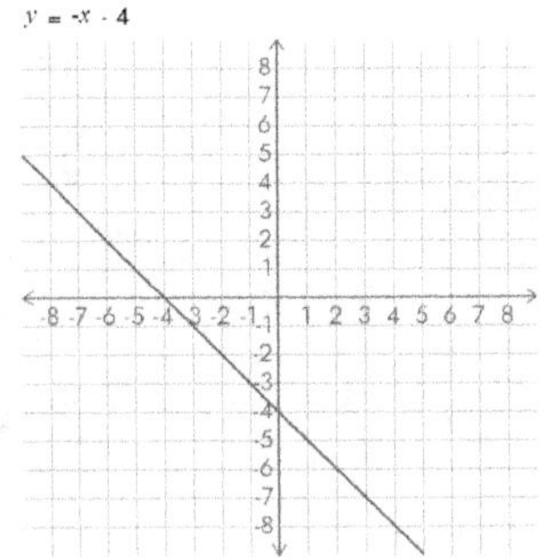

## Page 58:  Plotting Lines

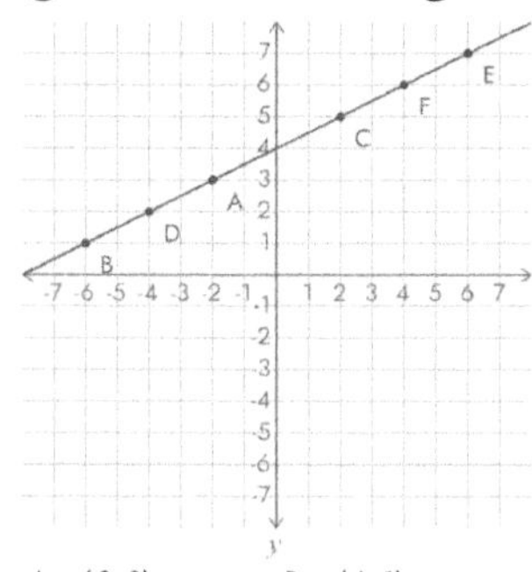

**1.**

A = (-2, 3)      B = (-6, 1)

C = (2, 5)       D = (-4, 2)

E = (6, 7)       F = (4, 6)

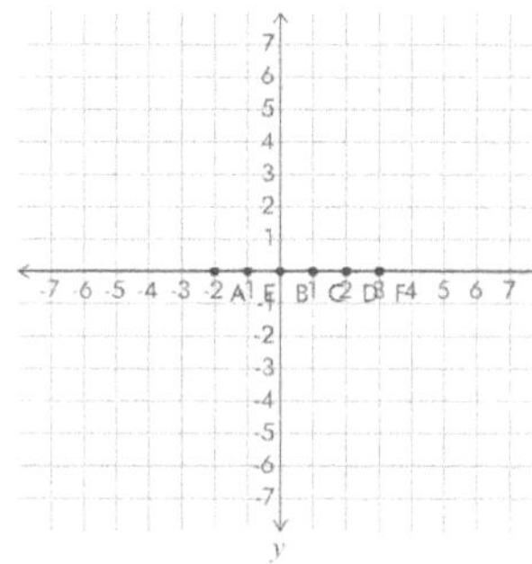

**2.**

A = (-2, 0)      B = (0, 0)

C = (1, 0)       D = (2, 0)

E = (-1, 0)      F = (3, 0)

**3.**

A = (-2, 4)      B = (-3, 6)

C = (0, 0)       D = (2, -4)

E = (-1, 2)      F = (1, -2)

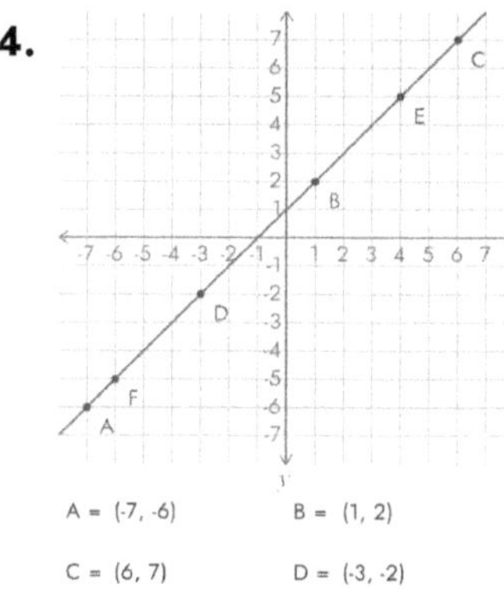

**4.**

A = (-7, -6)     B = (1, 2)

C = (6, 7)       D = (-3, -2)

E = (4, 5)       F = (-6, -5)

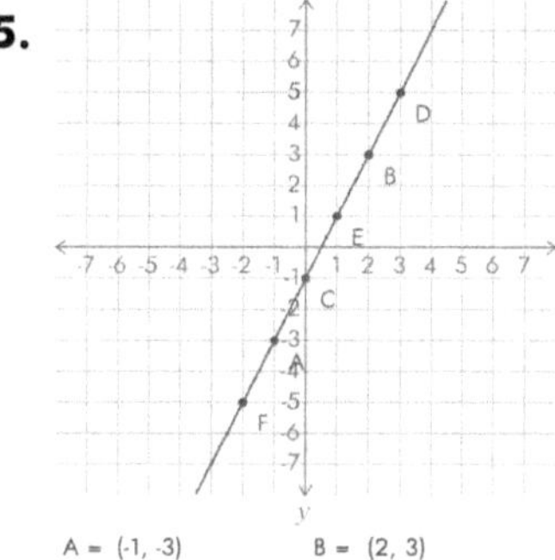

**5.**

A = (-1, -3)     B = (2, 3)

C = (0, -1)      D = (3, 5)

E = (1, 1)       F = (-2, -5)

## Page 63: Quadratic Equations

1. No real solution.
2. (2, -0.333)
3. (1.732, -1.732)
4. (2.178, -1.378)
5. (-2.708, 2.708)
6. (7, -3)
7. (8, -8)
8. (-1.876, 1.447)
9. (0.816, -0.816)
10. (1.683, -0.255)
11. (4.5, -4)
12. (-3, 2.667)
13. (2.135, -0.468)
14. (-2, 1.25)
15. (0.743, -1.834)
16. (-0.305, 1.638)
17. (3, -5.25)
18. (1.113, -1.946)

www.ingramcontent.com/pod-product-compliance
Lightning Source LLC
Chambersburg PA
CBHW081950160726
47999CB00008B/2571